In the Park

Written by Ruth Thomson
Illustrated by Jolyne Knox

PUBLISHED BY THE READER'S DIGEST ASSOCIATION LIMITED

One night, Daddy read Steve and Judy a very exciting bedtime story. It was all about an explorer who travelled to colourful, far-away places.

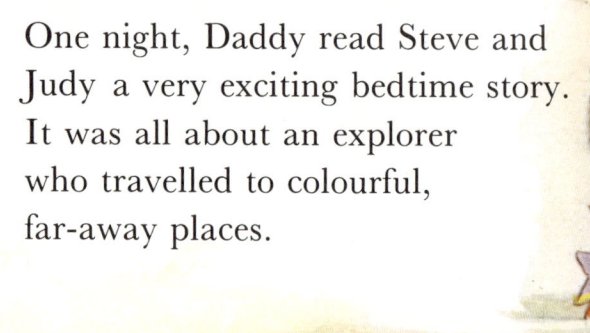

He cut a trail
through thick green jungle,
where red and orange flowers grew.

He crossed muddy brown rivers
on a raft made of tree trunks,
keeping a wary look-out
for snapping crocodiles.

On and on he travelled,
all in search of rare butterflies
that were every colour
you could imagine.

"I'd like to be an explorer," said Judy.
"Me too," said Steve.
"I've got an idea," said Daddy. "How about going on a trip to the park? I don't think we'll find many rare butterflies. Instead, we could see how many different coloured things we can find."

Early next morning,
the whole family set out for the park.
As they walked along the path,
Daddy suddenly said, "I spy
with my little eye, something red."

"The flowers," said Judy.
"That runner's tracksuit," said Mummy.
"No," said Daddy, "can you see something else that's red?"

"I know," said Judy,
"it's the kite."
She pointed upwards to the sky.

"I've found a red ladybird,"
said Steve, stooping down.

The path wound round an open space.
"I spy with my little eye,"
said Judy, "something green."
"But everything is green,"
said Steve, "the grass, the leaves,
the bushes and the trees."
"*This* is very dark green,"
said Judy, giving them an extra clue.

"It's the monkey-puzzle tree," exclaimed Mummy. "That's the darkest green tree I know."
"It's impossible to climb," said Steve. "That must be why it's called a monkey-puzzle tree."

In the middle of the open space, some children were playing football. "Come on the blues," yelled Steve, as he passed by.

"Up the oranges," called Judy, not to be outdone.

"Hurry up, you two," said Daddy, "Mummy's found something to show you."

"I spy with my little eye," began
Mummy, putting her finger to her lips,
"something grey; but don't move
or you'll frighten it away."
Judy and Steve stood as still
as statues.

"It's a squirrel," Judy whispered
as the bushy-tailed animal scampered
across the path.
"Aren't we lucky to see one!"

"Look," said Steve, following
the squirrel.
"There's the boating pond.
Can we have a go, please?"
"Of course," said Daddy.
"Which colour boat shall we have?"
The yellow one was too small,
the black one had a leak
and so they settled for the blue one.

They climbed in and rowed
to the middle of the pond.
"I spy with my little eye,"
said Steve, "something brown."

"The oars," suggested Mummy.
"The wooden bridge," said Judy.
"Wrong," said Steve. "What else is brown?"

"The ducks of course," laughed Daddy, splashing with the oars.

"Where to next?" said Judy,
when their time on the boat was up.
"Let's go through the rose garden.

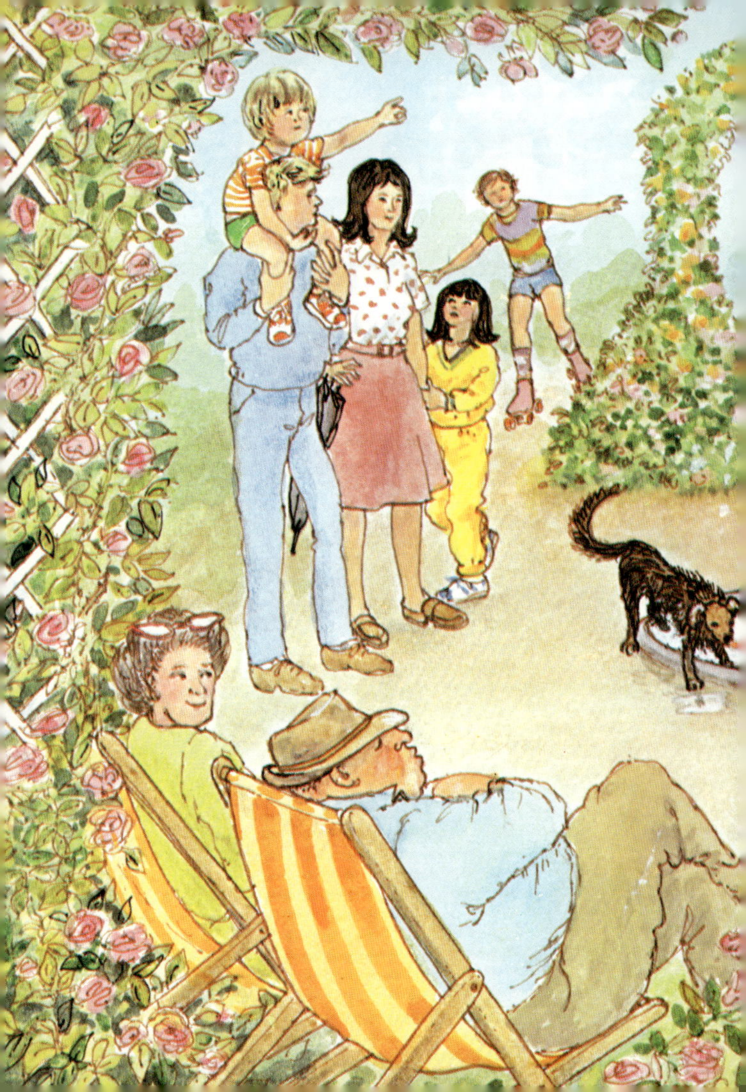

That's sure to be colourful," said Daddy.

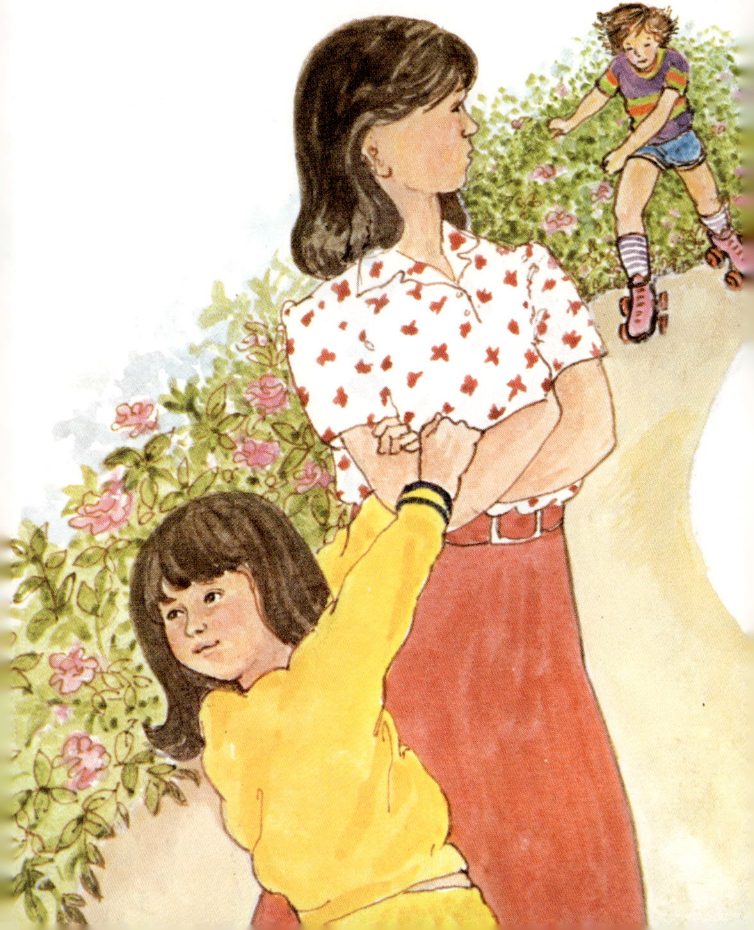

"I spy with my little eye
something pink," said Mummy.
"The roses, the roses,"
shouted Steve.
"That would be too easy,"
laughed Mummy.
"Look around you."

"It's the roller-skates,"
said Judy, stepping back
to let the skater past.

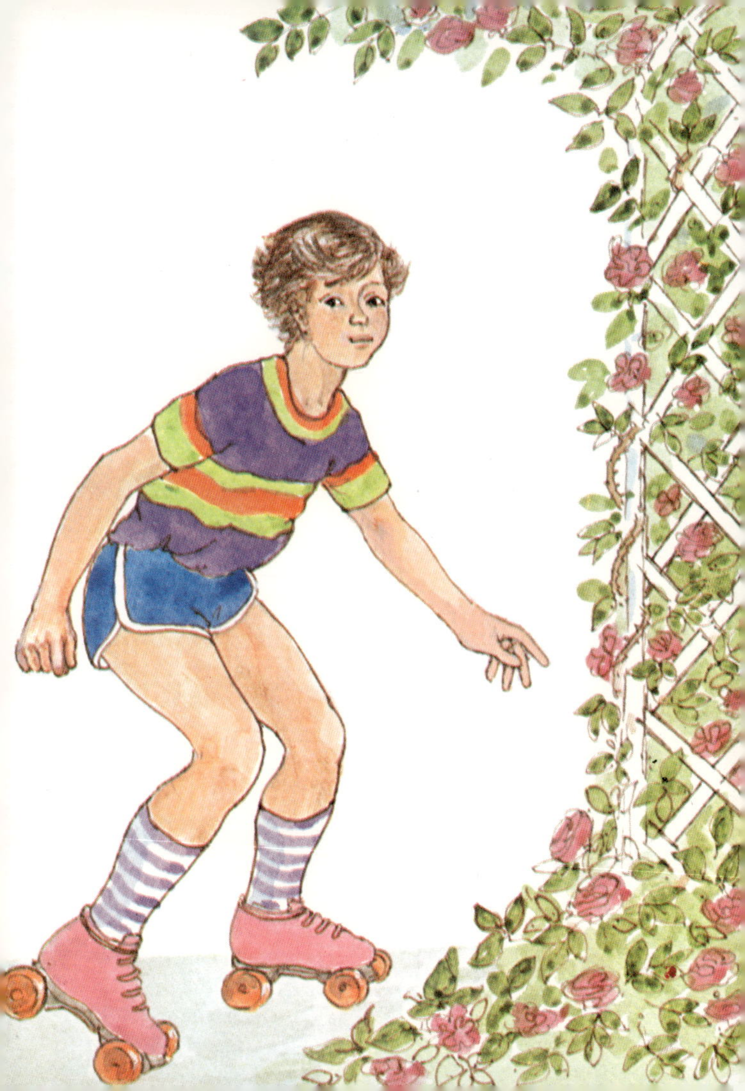

"Let's go this way now,"
said Steve, pointing to a bandstand
in the far distance.
"I spy with my little eye
something black," he said.
"The railings," said Daddy.
"The litter-bin," said Mummy.
"I'll give you another clue,"
said Steve, "it's moving."

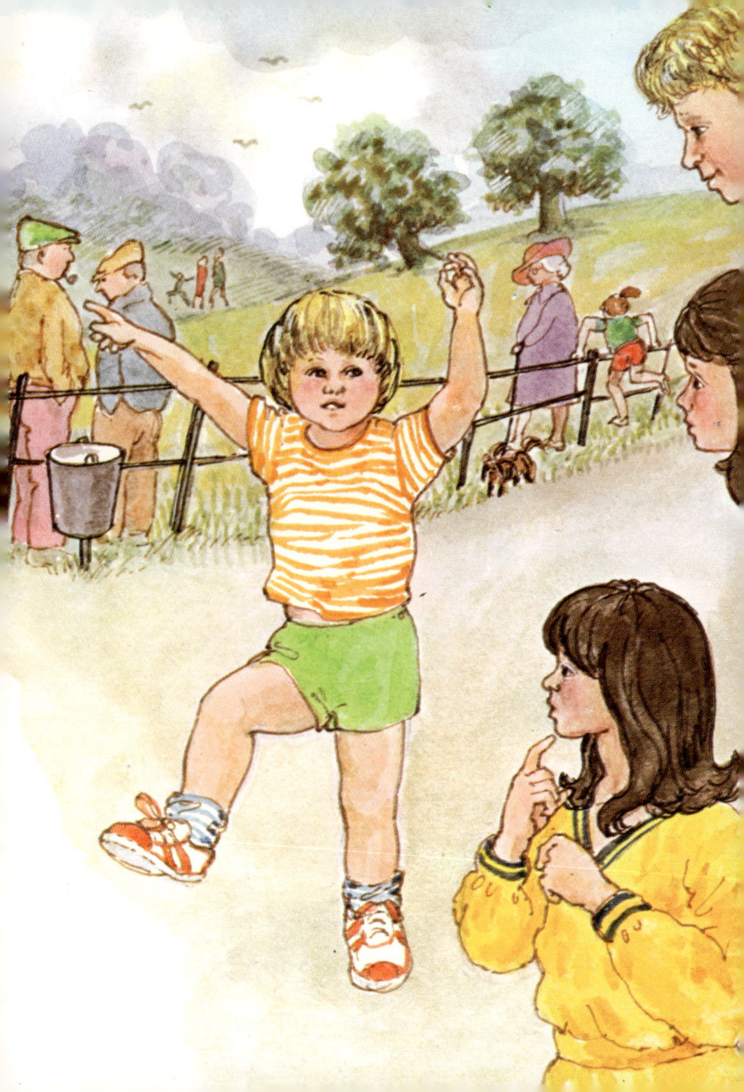

"It's that big dog," said Judy,
watching it run after a rubber ball.

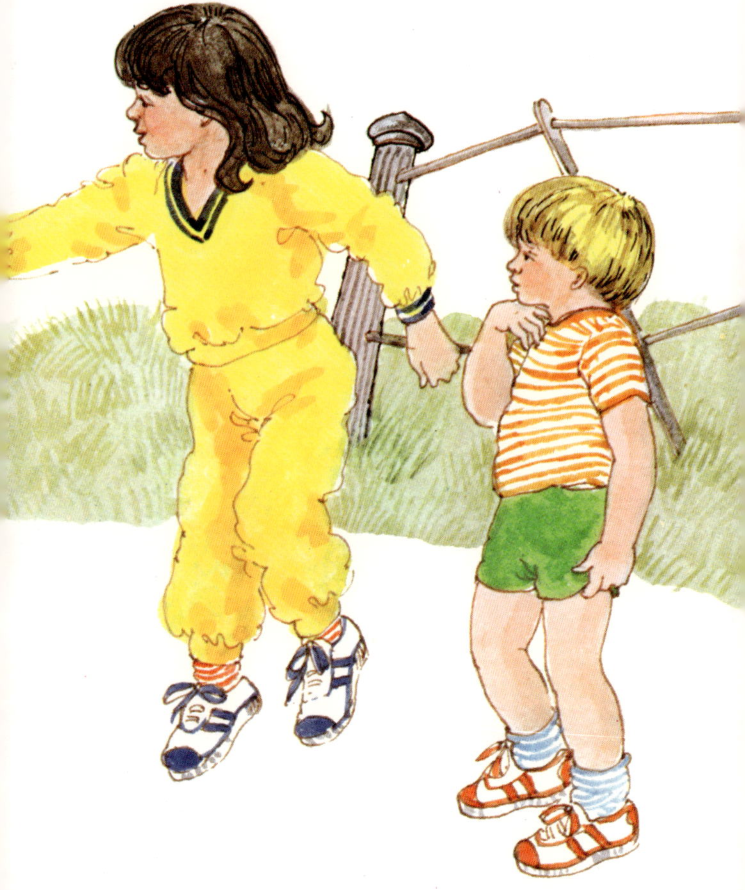

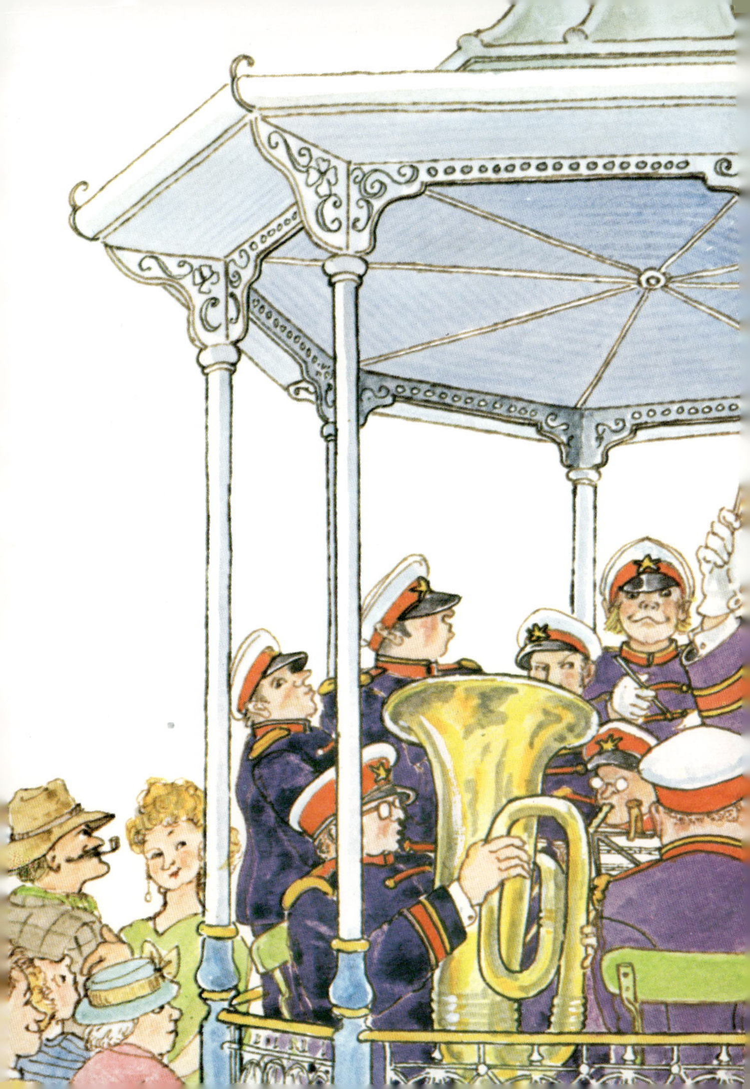

The family went up to the bandstand.
Its fresh white paint gleamed.
The band, dressed in smart purple uniforms, stood ready to play.
The conductor raised his baton.

There was a loud roll on the drums,
or that's what it sounded like.
But the drummer hadn't moved
a muscle.

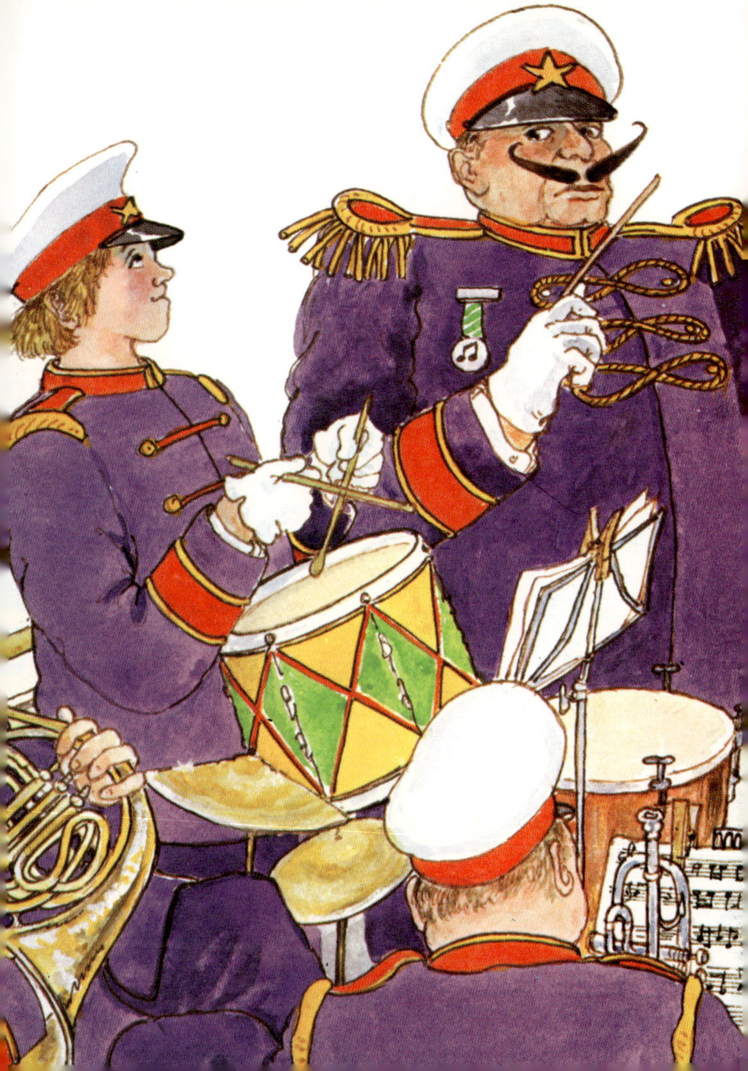

Everyone looked up at the sky.
It had turned a very nasty grey.
The thunder rolled again.

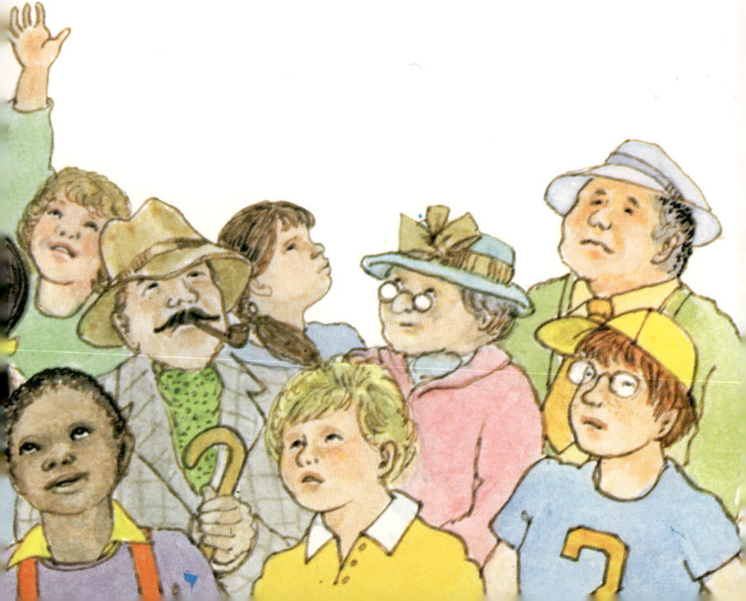

The sky blackened
and the rain began to pour.
Now there was almost no colour
at all.

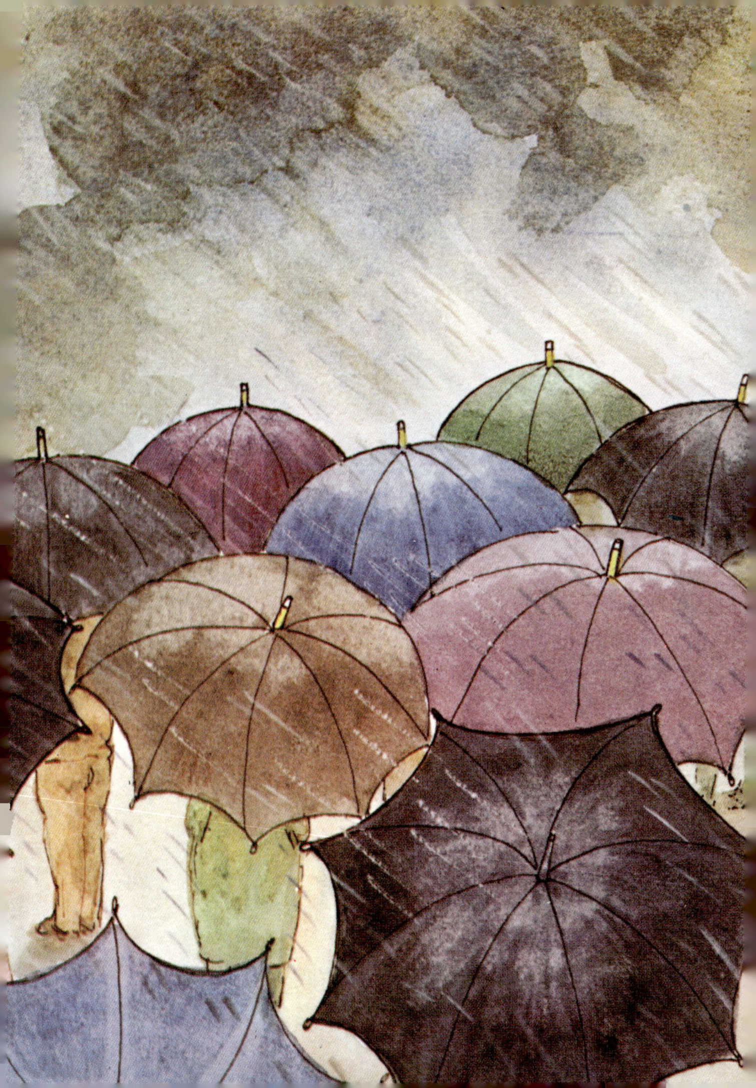

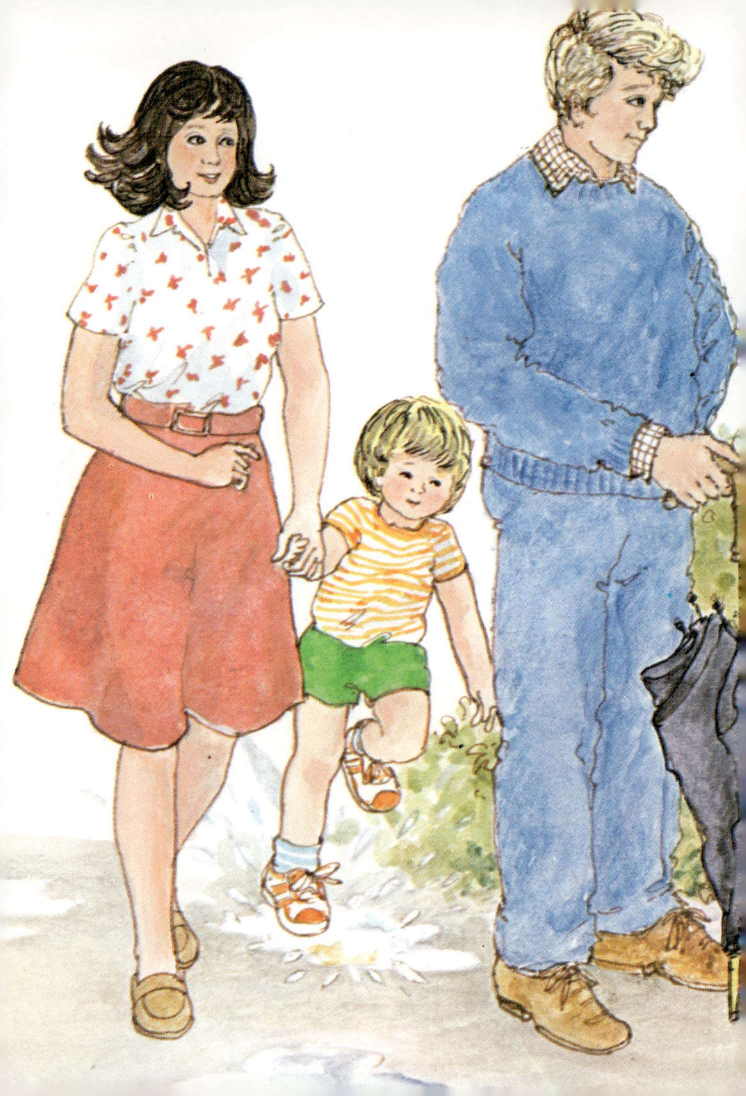

When the rain stopped,
Steve and Judy and Daddy and Mummy
walked back towards the park gates.
"Look," said Judy, "there's the most
colourful thing of all.
It's nearly as colourful
as all the things in the jungle."
They all stopped to see
what she was looking at.

It was a rainbow.
"Now we really have seen everything," said Steve. "What a day out!"

MY HOLIDAY LIBRARY

First Edition Copyright © 1983
Reprinted 1984
The Reader's Digest Association
Limited,
25 Berkeley Square, London W1X 6AB

All rights reserved.

® READER'S DIGEST
is a registered trademark of
The Reader's Digest Association, Inc.
of Pleasantville, New York, U.S.A.

Phototypeset by Tradespools Limited,
Frome, Somerset
Printed in Hong Kong